the private life of

the cat who...

Also by Lilian Jackson Braun

e

SHORT STORY COLLECTIONS

the private life of
the cat who…

Tales of Koko and Yum Yum
from the Journal of
James Mackintosh Qwilleran

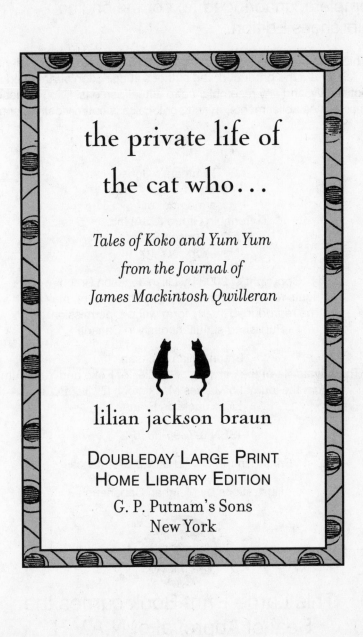

lilian jackson braun

DOUBLEDAY LARGE PRINT
HOME LIBRARY EDITION

G. P. Putnam's Sons
New York

This Large Print Edition, prepared especially for Doubleday Large Print Home Library, contains the complete, unabridged text of the original Publisher's Edition.

G. P. Putnam's Sons
Publishers Since 1838
a member of
Penguin Group (USA) Inc.
375 Hudson Street
New York, NY 10014

Braun, Lilian Jackson.
The private life of the cat who . . . : tales of Koko and Yum Yum from the journal of James Mackintosh Qwilleran / by Lilian Jackson Braun.

ISBN 0-7394-3916-2

Printed in the United States of America

Illustrations by Meighan Cabanaugh

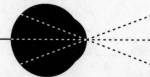

This Large Print Book carries the Seal of Approval of N.A.V.H.

Dedicated to Earl Bettinger
The Husband Who . . .

contents

〜

foreword

James Mackintosh Qwilleran is a journalist who wrote for metropolitan newspapers from coast to coast before relocating in Pickax City, four hundred miles north of everywhere. Now he writes a twice-weekly column for *The Moose County Something,* and also keeps a personal journal of his off-duty experiences.

Koko is a "real cool cat" who happens to have sixty whiskers instead of the usual forty-eight. Yum Yum the Paw, as she is known, is an adorable female who will steal anything—including hearts.

These excerpts from Qwilleran's journal include memories, thoughts, and ideas from the "Qwill Pen" column. Altogether it's a drama starring two feline celebrities.

Raise the curtain!

the private life of
the cat who...

1.

enter:
kao k'o kung, howling

I'll never forget those days! I was getting my life back on track. I had a job, writing features for the *Daily Fluxion.* I had a place to live, an apartment on the ground floor of an old mansion. And soon I would be getting a roommate!

My landlord, who was art critic for the *Fluxion,* lived upstairs with his art treasures and a Siamese called Kao K'o Kung. Although I knew nothing about cats, I was enlisted for cat-sitting when the critic was out of town.

He wrote his reviews at home and never went near the news office. According to conventional wisdom, he never went near the art galleries either, but wrote his nasty criticism off the top of his head. Among local artists he was well hated, to coin a phrase. So no one was surprised when he was murdered in his own backyard.

That was the first time I heard the cat's "death howl," a blood-curdling experience!

Kao K'o Kung—that smart cat!—then walked downstairs and moved in with me. I recall giving him some turkey from the Press Club that I had been saving for myself.

So here we were! Thrown together by fate! First thing I did, I changed his name to Koko.

He made no objection. He knew which side his bread was buttered on! In the days that followed we invented games to play, both athletic and intellectual. I was at work all day but made up for it by reading to him every evening—either the *Daily Fluxion* or the dictionary; he was not particular.

Then I began to find fault with the old mansion. It seemed to be the ancestral domain of a dynasty of moths, which were eating holes in my bathrobe and neckties. But where could I move? Apartments in my price range specified "no pets allowed." I discussed the problem with Koko, who listened thoughtfully. I told him that a friend of mine was going to Europe for three months and had suggested that I house-sit. Koko squeezed his eyes. We were getting to be pals. Then, to my surprise, he turned out be a self-appointed bodyguard and somewhat of a bloodhound!

One day he wanted to go upstairs to his old haunt. The murdered man's treasures had been removed, but I had a key to the apartment and the supply of cat litter. But that cat seemed to have his own urgent reason; he ran up and down the stairs ahead of me in anticipation.

Sure enough, there was a large tapestry still hanging in a hallway, and Koko was determined to paw his way behind it. When I went to his assistance, I discovered a door back there, which the landlord had found it advisable to conceal. It led downstairs to a small ground-floor apartment in the rear of the building, and it was filled with clues to the recent crime. It had been used as an artist's studio and still had an odor of turpentine.

Just as I was snooping around in amazement and Koko was getting some kind of catly high from the paintbrushes, I heard a key turn in the rear door leading to the backyard, and a big man walked in. For a moment we were both frozen in surprise. Then he looked about wildly, grabbed a palette knife, and came at me!

Before I could find a chair to swing at him, Koko threw a catfit! The room seemed filled with snarling animals, attacking him from all sides with claws extended! I was able to clobber the guy, and we left him on the floor while we called the police. Koko spent the next few hours licking his claws.

⁓

I was glad to move into my friend's posh apartment on the fifteenth floor of the Villa Verandah. Koko seemed happy, too. I think he liked the view. Then one day I came home from work and found a large hole in the green wool upholstery of a fine wing chair. As I examined it, with horror, Koko jumped onto the chair seat and upchucked a green fur ball—still moist!

I immediately phoned the Press Club bartender, who always had the answer to all questions.

He listened and said wisely, "Sounds like an emotional problem. You need a psycatatrist. I can tell you where to find one."

It sounded like a hoax, especially since the address he gave me was on the edge of the red-light district. And I was even more suspicious when I phoned for an appointment and was told to come alone without the cat . . . but I was desperate! I reported for the consultation.

It was a tawdry house, but there were cats on every windowsill, and that was promising. I was welcomed by a kindly woman in a faded housedress accompanied by at least a dozen cats who seemed quite well adjusted. She ushered me into the parlor and gave me a cup of tea with the inevitable cat hair floating in it. No matter.

What I learned, after stating the problem, was this: Siamese, when troubled, become wool eaters. My ties and bathrobe were undoubtedly wool. Koko was lonely because he was accustomed to having someone at home all day. He needed a nice little Siamese female for a companion. Neutering would make no difference. They would be quite sweet to each other. . . . I found this concept extremely interesting.

Now all I had to do was find a little female Siamese. . . .

Panic time! Here I was—a lifelong cat illiterate—involved in matchmaking between temperamental Siamese! I phoned the Press Club bartender for advice once more.

"Call the catteries listed in the Yellow Pages," he said with authority. "Check the classified ads in the paper. Call the pet hospitals!"

I did. My efforts turned up only one available candidate, and the asking price was more than my weekly paycheck at the *Fluxion*. I was just getting back on my feet financially. I needed to make a down payment on a used car.

Meanwhile I was afraid to leave Koko alone in the borrowed apartment; he might start eating the rugs! Once, as a test, I shut him up in the bathroom, and he howled so continuously and with such volume that there were five complaints to the manager.

Someone suggested selling Koko; it would solve the whole problem.

I considered that unthinkable. Already I

felt a kinship with him that was hard to explain.

I'll never forget the frantic search for a
companion who would stop Koko from eating wool!

2.

enter:
yum yum, shrieking

She was a poor little rich cat when I first met her. Didn't even know her name. And she was the butt of arguments between husband and wife. He hated cats. She sat in a wheelchair all day, stroking the kitten on her lap. The little thing was a Siamese, she said, but so young that her brown points had not appeared. There was only a brown splotch on her nose. Her name was Freya, the woman said.

The man, a jade collector, said her name was Yu, an Asian word for jade. I thought it was a ridiculous name for a cat. How would you call her? You'd have to say, "Hey, Yu!"

I had gone there with a photographer to get a story on a fine old house that had been updated by a fine young designer. The Taits were supposed to be a fine old family, but there were signs that the family fortune had been squandered by the jade collector. Altogether, it was not a pleasant experience, but the photos were excellent, and it made a good story.

Twenty-four hours after it came out, there was a scandalous development: burglary, sudden death, missing person, rumors of fraud, even murder.

By this time, Koko had upchucked the memorable green fur ball, and I was searching for a female Siamese. I phoned the Tait house and learned that the poor little creature had been thrown out. Thrown out! Gulp.

How she was rescued is another story. The facts are that I brought her home in a taxi; Koko was with me. We had a cardboard carton with air holes punched in the sides. I talked to her. Told her that her name was Yum Yum. She was quiet except when we turned a corner or passed a truck or stopped for a red light or exceeded fifty miles per hour. Then she would make a sudden ear-splitting screech that made it difficult for the taxi driver to keep his vehicle on the road.

At the Villa Verandah, when we went up to the fifteenth floor in the elevator, the ascent did something to her littler interior; her piercing shriek made women faint and strong men wince.

All that is over now. Yum Yum is happy. Koko has stopped eating wool.

We've been together several years now and the little girl has grown into a charming young lady—with some playful idiosyncrasies, like untying shoelaces, stealing small shiny objects, and losing her toys. It's obvious that I'm smitten with the poor little rich cat. So are the readers of my column in *The Moose County Something.*

She still utters a shriek when it's least expected. But who could resist her winsome ways?

When I'm reading, she climbs up on the back of my chair and breathes hotly into my ear and then bites it ever so gently.

When I'm reading aloud, she puts her ear against my chest and purrs. She identifies the resonance, my vet explained, with her mother's breathing when she was in her womb. I don't tell that to everyone.

3.

confessions of a cat-illiterate

Early in life my education in pet culture was sadly neglected. A dog said "woof" and a cat said "meow"; that was all I knew or cared to know. Not until middle age did I come face-to-face with the breed of feline called Siamese.

Koko has a yowl at a decibel level sufficient to knock you over, and Yum Yum has a soprano shriek like a knife in the eardrum. Not all the time, of course. Under ordinary circumstances their conversation can be quite civilized.

Koko has moments of irritability when he chatters "ik ik ik" as a royal put-down. (He knows—even if no one else does—that he is descended from the royal cats of ancient Siam.)

Yum Yum's vocabulary was limited to a timid "mm-m-m" when she first came to live with us; her role as lap cat for an invalid had dictated a certain sickroom reserve. Eventually she learned "yow" from Koko—a fine all-purpose syllable that lends itself to a variety of meanings. The knife-like "EEEK" is her own idea. Thus far, no fatalities have been attributed to it.

Yum Yum has one original expression that is demanding and yet sweetly definite at the same time. According to women friends, its onset coincided with the feminist movement. Yum Yum says, "N-N-NOW."

4.

the cat who had
60 whiskers

From the very beginning I knew Koko was a remarkable cat. But his gifts continue to amaze me—and mystify me! Then I read somewhere that cats have forty-eight whiskers, including those feelers above the eyes that I call eyebrows. When I convinced that little devil to let me count his whiskers, I came up with a total of sixty! My journalist's skepticism demanded a recount. . . . Sixty!

Most cats, I'm told, are nervous before a violent storm, and they're being used to predict earthquakes. We have no earthquakes in this area, but Koko has a tantrum before a storm. What's more, he is visibly disturbed when an intruder is approaching.

He lets me know, several seconds in advance, when the phone is about to ring— and whether to expect friend or foe. How does he know?

One more puzzlement: He senses right from wrong! Not only when a faucet is dripping or the light has been left on in the broom closet; that little four-legged psychic knows good from evil.

These are facts I have confided to only two or three persons, knowing that my close friends would decide I was cracking up.

How Koko conveys his information seems too far-fetched to believe, and really must be attributed to coincidence. He licks glossy photographs, pushes books off the shelf, and swipes small objects with bold impudence. Whenever this occurs, his bizarre action steers my mind in a certain direction. Since I often have my own suspicions, it's possible to put two and two together.

My source of personal hunches, strangely, is a tremor on the upper lip, causing me to pound my mustache. I've been kidded about my overgrown mustache for years, and it has become part of my persona. Now I wonder if it helps me tune in to

Koko's extrasensory perception. I'm serious! Koko's sixty whiskers may be the catly equivalent of the optic fibers that carry information in today's digital world.

Kao K'o Kung has ESP
And a higher IQ than you and me.
He loafs all day
And has a devious way
Of getting his gourmet meals for free!

5.

yum yum the paw

Everyone admires Koko, but everyone loves Yum Yum! She's so dainty, so kittenish, so sweet! But don't be fooled! She has a mind of her own . . . and a talent for larceny! You see, she has this lightning-quick paw that darts out silently and pilfers some small shiny object. Over a period of time her loot has included a silver pen, a gold watch, a guest's lipstick, a silver cigarette lighter, and another guest's left earring, pulled off when she used the phone and found under the sofa several weeks later.

The police chief visits us occasionally, and Yum Yum has designs on his badge but contents herself by untying his shoelaces.

She stole my toothbrush twice before I

learned to keep it under lock and key. She is fascinated by brushes, including the one on my upper lip. The famous paw reaches out and touches my mustache with wonder—this when I'm in my lounge chair and she's perched on my chest.

Speaking of toothbrushes, I recall an incident one winter when we were living in Junktown—a street of Victorian town houses occupied by antique shops, with studio apartments upstairs. I was writing a series on Junktown and rented a second-floor-rear for a few months. It had been owned by a famous editor and abolitionist in the nineteenth century. The cats were fascinated by the pigeons in the backyard; I was fascinated by the extensive bookshelves and quantity of old books.

One day a toothbrush (not mine) appeared in the middle of the floor. Yum Yum looked guilty but refused to answer questions. I threw the toothbrush away.

A few days later, I was visiting my neighbor in second-floor-front when I noticed a red feather on the carpet. It was my feather! It had recently disappeared from the brim of my tweed porkpie! You see, in the nineteenth century the house had been a part of the Underground Railroad, harboring run-away slaves. There was a tunnel concealed in the bookcases, and Yum Yum had sneaked through, exchanging my feather for my neighbor's toothbrush!

Now Yum Yum amuses herself by stealing one of my socks, wrestling with it, beating it up, then losing it. I have a drawer full of socks without mates. If I throw them out, the missing ones will suddenly appear.

But I can think of one act of heroism for which her famous paw must be given credit. We were spending some time at the beach, and a hummingbird flew smack into a porch screen, getting its long slender bill caught in the mesh. Yum Yum, huddled on a porch table, calmly stood on her hind legs and gave the trapped bill a whack with her paw. The bird flew away, and she went back to dreaming about silver thimbles and toothbrushes.

6.

koko and the siamese rope trick

This happened after the Great Jade Robbery, following my feature on the Tait mansion. In the *Fluxion* photo lab, the pundits who claim to have the inside dirt on everything maintained that there was no robbery. It was a hoax engineered by Tait himself in order to collect on his insurance and embarrass the *Daily Fluxion*. Tait had family connections with our competitor and a longtime grudge against the *Flux.*

The photographer who had worked on the assignment with me had an idea. He knew I was going to pick up the Taits' cat. He would give me a set of prints—close-ups, of the jades and shots of the house interior. It would be a friendly gesture and would give me a chance to snoop a little. I was going solely to pick up the cat and was taking Koko to help ease the transition.

The photos were handsome shots, printed eleven-by-fourteen, with bleeding edges. As I spread out the interior views and studied them, Koko sneaked up and licked one of them.

"No!" I thundered. It was probably the only time in his life that he had been scolded. He glared at me and then left the room in what might be called high dudgeon.

The photo he blistered with his saliva was a shot of a breakfront that had been in the Tait family for generations. The detail was excellent; the grain of the wood, the lead mullions of the glass doors, and even the hairline shadows where the wood was joined. I could only hope that Tait wouldn't notice the blistered photo.

I apologized to Koko, buckled him into his harness, and attached the length of rope that would have to serve as a leash until I could buy one. Then I hailed a taxi. At the Tait house I told the driver to wait.

He said, "You with the *Flux*? I recognized the mustache." Cabdrivers feel a camaraderie with newsmen.

To make a long story short, Tait was over-
joyed. As soon as he left to get the kitten, I
set Koko down on the floor—and played
out the rope as he walked directly to the
heirloom breakfront and sniffed the hairline
crack that had shown up in the photo. It
was in the side of the large cabinet. I
touched the crack, and the section opened.

Before I could identify the contents of the
secret compartment, Tait was coming at me
with a jade harpoon. Next thing I knew, he
was on the floor unable to move. The cat
had flown around and around trussing the
man's legs in the rope leash, and he contin-
ued to guard him with bared fangs and
menacing snarls until the police came.

The little female was on top of the breakfront, gazing down and wondering, perhaps, what kind of family she was joining.

7.

yum yum and the interior designer

When I inherited the Klingenschoen fortune and moved to Pickax with my two suitcases and two Siamese cats, police chief Andrew Brodie gave me some astute advice in his slightly Scottish brogue: "Look sharp, laddie! All the women in town will be after you and your money."

His daughter, Fran Brodie, was among the first. She was an interior designer—with strawberry blond hair, a model's figure, gorgeous legs, and she always wore those high-heeled flimsy sandals, in and out of season.

My plan was to donate the sumptuous Klingenschoen mansion to the historical society and live in the servants' quarters in the

carriage house. I commissioned Fran to fur-
nish the rooms in Comfortable Contempo-
rary. The project called for numerous con-
sultations, sitting side by side on the old
Depression-era sofa with furniture cata-
logues and large books of fabric swatches
spread out on our knees.

"No, I don't want a four-poster bed," I
told her. "No, I don't want pleated fabric on
the walls. No, I don't want a mirrored ceiling."

These appointments were always made
in late afternoon, after which I was obliged
to offer her a cocktail, after which I was
more or less obliged to take her to dinner.
She suggested a cozy trip to Chicago to
visit furniture showrooms.

All I wanted was a comfortable environ-
ment in which to live and work. To tell the
truth, I had never liked sexually aggressive
females, no matter how classy their legs. I
preferred to do my own chasing. As for the
Siamese, they seemed to sense that Fran
was lukewarm about cats. In fact, Yum Yum
was patently possessive of me, hovering
close and staring with a go-home look in
her eyes. That's a "look" that Siamese do
very well.

"Why is that cat following me around?" Fran demanded while measuring wall spaces.

"She's responding to your magnetic personality," I said. "Have you thought of a way to display my antique Mackintosh crest?" It was currently leaning against the wall of the foyer—a round ornament of wrought iron a yard in diameter.

"It's somewhat out of scale, you know. But . . . it might be possible to use it as camouflage for that big ugly radiator."

A few days later I came home in late afternoon and saw Fran's car in the parking lot. She had a key to the apartment and sometimes dropped in to take measurements or work on floor plans.

Walking up the narrow stairs I noticed that the Mackintosh crest was no longer leaning against the wall. Good! That meant she had found a way to display it.

"Hello!" I shouted, but there was no reply.

In the living room, the crest was lying in the middle of the floor, and two cats were huddled over it in attitudes of troubled concern.

"What happened! Where is she?" I demanded.

Then I noticed a red light on the answering machine. "This is Fran. Call me at home."

"Oh, Qwill! You'll never guess what happened! I had an idea for the Mackintosh crest and was taking it over to the radiator to see how it looked . . ."

"You didn't try to lift that thing!" I interrupted.

"No, I was rolling it like a hoop, and I stepped on a cat's tail! There was such a hair-raising screech that I rolled the crest over my foot."

"I hope you weren't hurt!"

"Hurt? I broke three toes! A police car took me to the hospital . . . so we'll have to call off the Chicago trip."

I was much relieved. I had no desire to traipse through furniture showrooms in Chicago. I said, "Which one of you rascals caused the accident?"

Koko looked noncommittal. Yum Yum was licking her paw and washing her face.

8.

koko and the rum tum tugger syndrome

In *Old Possum's Book of Practical Cats,* the author, T. S. Eliot, talks about a cat named Rum Tum Tugger: *For he will do / As he do do / And there's no doing anything about it!*

I wish to go on record as saying that Kao K'o Kung is Rum Tum Tugger the Second.

I knew from the beginning that he had his own ideas, but it was not until the episode of the Pork Liver Cupcakes that I could definitely accuse him of Rum Tum Tuggerism.

A friend of ours, Hixie Rice—nice girl but a little wacky—knew a chef who wanted to develop a line of Frozen Foods for Fussy Felines. To promote it, Hixie envisioned a video in which Koko would endorse the product. At the time we were living in the old Klin-

genschoen mansion with its crystal chande-
liers, grand staircase, and K monogram on
everything monogrammable.

The synopsis was simple. With the camera grinding at the foot of the stairs, Koko
would be shown at the top of the flight.
Then he would run downstairs on cue and
into the dining room, where a plate of pork
liver cupcakes awaited on a K-mono-
grammed plate. (K for Koko. Get it?)

Hixie was at the bottom of the stairs with
the camera; I was at the top with Koko, who
was supposed to look alert and eager and
hungry. Unfortunately he had just stuffed
himself with diced prime rib with a side of
Roquefort cheese, and he felt like taking a
nap. In fact, he was lying on his side, looking blotto.

Hixie called from the foot of the stairs,
"Stand him up on four legs!"

I said, "You come up and stand him on
four legs, and I'll take the pictures."

With some changes in the scenario and a
gentle shove to his rear end, he flew down
the stairs and over the head of the photographer.

When I finally grabbed the struggling,
kicking model, Hixie was willing to settle for

a close-up of him gobbling the evil-looking smear of gray pork liver on a K plate. Koko took one look at it and bushed his tail, looking at the camera with ears back, nose wrinkled, and fangs bared in an expression of utter revulsion. End of publicity shoot.

e

Over the years I've come to the conclusion that Koko considers picture-taking an invasion of his privacy. He's so handsome, though, that I can't be blamed for wanting a portrait. Yet even John Bushland, a professional of the highest order, was unable to shoot Rum Tum Tugger.

Despite several attempts, using all the tricks of the trade, Bushy has still been unsuccessful. "I haven't given up!" he said. "One of these days I'll get that little devil!"

That's what he thinks. Koko is a Rum Tum Tugger. Yum Yum, yes. Koko, no!

Bushy, as we all call him, said one day that he'd like to photograph Koko and Yum Yum for a cat calendar. He suggested that I take them to his studio in Lockmaster. I didn't want to discourage him, so I agreed, and we drove down there on a Saturday morning.

The cats were on the backseat in their usual travel coop with a cushion and a door at one end. I could tell, by the way they both huddled at the back of the coop, that they knew some dire experience was in store for them. I talked reassuringly to them as I drove, but I could feel the bad vibes coming my way.

I had suggested to Bushy that we keep our voices low and leave them in their carrier while we had a cup of coffee and talked about the weather.

This we did. Then, making sure to close both exit doors, we casually opened the carrier door and had another cup of coffee. The cats remained on their cushion.

After a while I said, "You get your camera ready, and I'll casually draw one out; the other will follow. The whole idea is to stay calm."

They were both crammed together at the rear of the conveyance, but I reached in and got a handful of fur. It was Koko, bracing himself against the sides of the carrier. He had the strength of an iron vise. No way was that cat going to go through that small door.

"How're you doing?" Bushy asked quietly.

"Batting zero," I said under my breath. I and Koko were both very quiet and unruffled. He didn't protest, just braced himself against the sides of the opening.

"He doesn't wanna and he ain't gonna," I said.

"Leave him alone and leave the door open. We'll have another cup of coffee," Bushy said. "He'll saunter out of his own accord."

We drank a lot of the brew that morning and discussed every topic in the news, but Koko never sauntered out. He was doing his Rum Tum Tugger act, and as T. S. Eliot said: *There's no doing anything about it!*

9.

cats! who can understand them?

When Koko and Yum Yum came to live with me, I was a novice about cat care. No on had told me how to be personal valet, gourmet caterer, and wise parent to a pair of pampered Siamese. Perhaps "pampered" is the wrong word. What I mean to say . . . They had definite opinions of their own on every matter that came to the fore.

Vitamin pills, for example. No one at the pet shop told me how to administer the formidable tablets. I consulted my neighbor, Rosemary Whiting, who had raised, successfully, cats, dogs, and children.

"Simple!" she said. "I'll demonstrate."

First, I learned, you catch the cat, who has become an expert at mind reading.

Rosemary knelt on the floor of the kitchenette with Koko between her knees. "The secret is: Stay calm," she said. "Tell him he's a good kitty. Stroke his fur. Gradually circle his head with your left hand, applying pressure to the hinge of the jaw. His mouth opens. You pop the pill down his gullet. Gently grasp his jaw to close his mouth while stroking his throat until he gulps. . . . Success!"

Koko had been cooperative and stayed between Rosemary's knees as if waiting for another pill.

"It's all in knowing how," she said. "Stay calm and the cat will relax."

At that point Koko gulped again and deposited the pill on the floor—damp but otherwise intact.

"Oops!" she said.

"He's relaxed, all right," I commented.

"No problem. We'll repeat the process, and it'll stay down. He'll get the idea."

She was right. The pill stayed down—for a couple of minutes. Then Koko heaved a convulsive burp and shot the pill into the adjoining living area, where it disappeared among the seat cushions.

See what I mean?

෴

Next, someone who seemed to know advised me to have Koko's teeth cleaned, saying that Siamese require dental prophylaxis oftener than other breeds. I made an appointment at the pet clinic.

Koko made no protest. He had been to the vet before and actually purred when his temperature was being taken. He seemed quite at home on the examination table until . . . a firm hand forced his mouth open.

Then, before the good doctor could assess the situation, Koko galvanized into a missile of catly energy. An assistant reached for the flailing legs. I yelled, "Koko!" and grabbed his lashing tail! But he turned inside out and somehow landed on top of an eight-foot cabinet, from which he glared down at his pursuers and uttered a tirade of Siamese curses. Anyone who has not been cussed out by an angry Siamese doesn't know what profanity is all about!

Oh yes, he jumped down after being ignored for a few minutes. He jumped down to the examination table and opened his mouth!

See what I mean? My theory is that cats in general and Siamese in particular have a wicked sense of humor. They enjoy making us look like fools.

10.

the matter of the silver thimble

It's like this: There are thousands of house cats, barn cats, and cat fanciers in Moose County, and readers of my "Qwill Pen" column enjoy hearing about the antics of the Siamese occasionally. They are awed by the handsome, intelligent Koko, but they love the sweet little Yum Yum with her dainty demeanor and iron will. In fact, there is a Yum Yum Fan Club in the county.

Members of this unofficial organization send her crocheted mice that squeak and plastic balls that rattle. Her most precious possession, though, is a silver thimble, a gift from a dear reader no longer able to sew. "Cats," she said, "love thimbles."

Yum Yum has always liked anything small and shiny, but she is absolutely infatuated with her thimble.

She bats it around with her delicate paw, carries it from one venue to another in her tiny teeth, hides it, forgets where it's hidden, then cries until I look under rugs, behind seat cushions, and in wastebaskets to retrieve it.

She has deposited it in the pockets of my jackets, in a bowl of mixed nuts, and down the drain of the kitchen sink.

I should take it away from her, but I haven't the heart. She would pine away and die.

Many of her playthings vanish, especially her dearly beloved silver thimble. In fact I've been moved to write a limerick in her honor:

Little Yum Yum is quite a cat!
She walks thin and sleeps fat.
One of her joys
Is losing her toys,
And she never knows where her
thimble's at!

I have appealed to readers of the news-paper. All solutions to the problem will be thoughtfully considered. Address me in care of the psychiatric ward at the Pickax General Hospital.

11.

cool koko's almanac

While researching Benjamin Franklin's life for column material, I was reminded of his wise sayings published as *Poor Richard's Almanack* and I thought, "Hey! Koko could steal his idea! Old Ben wouldn't mind; he had a sense of humor. . . ." Here's the first installment.

- A cat without a tail is better than a politician without a head.

- There's a destiny that leads a hungry cat to the right doorstep.

- Home is where the sardines are.

- No matter how humble, a free meal is not to be sniffed at.

- Where there's a will, a cat will find a way.

- Soft cushions are for cats—all others use them at their own risk.

- What goes down must come up, if it's a pill.

12.

why do cats do what they do?

When I started writing the "Qwill Pen" column for *The Moose County Something,* I envisioned a forum for ideas, book reviews, personality stories, and information on local occupations and hobbies. In a weak moment I happened to mention that I shared my domicile with two Siamese cats. Cat fanciers all over the county responded with newsworthy tales of their own feline housemates.

Moose County, I swear, has more cats per capita than any other county in the U.S. Readers asked questions about Koko and Yum Yum, wrote letters to Koko and Yum Yum, and otherwise developed a chummy rapport. Reader participation is always welcomed by small-town newspapers, but we had almost more than we wanted. Wherever I went, strangers shouted, "Hi, Mr. Q! How's Koko?" . . . "Did Yum Yum find her thimble?"

Thought-provoking topics were suggested for discussion: Why do cats do what they do? Do cats have a sense of humor? No hardworking columnist is averse to having readers share his workload, and some curious incidents were aired in the "Qwill Pen" column.

about toulouse

He was half-starved when he came to that particular doorstep in Indian Village. Did he sense that Mildred Riker was food writer for *The Moose County Something*?

He was a sad sight, she recalled, his fur matted with blood and mud, one bad ear, and a slight limp. We gave him a dish of tuna—not too much at first—we didn't want him to make himself sick. He didn't even sniff it! He stared for a moment—in what must have been disbelief—and then did something very curious. He raised his right front paw and did three pawing motions in the air before starting to eat, as if asking a blessing! It was so touching! Such a winning gesture! We adopted him at once.

Now, after a bath and a trip to the vet and a proper diet, he's a handsome black-and-white longhair. But here's the amazing thing! Before every meal he still paws the air three times!

about princess

From Purple Point comes an anonymous note:

Princess is pure white with four black feet and two black ears that she wears like a crown. I brought her with me when I visited my daughter. The guest bed was queen-size and had some designer bed sheets (Dior, as I recall). A most unusual design! Broad stripes in bold colors ran diagonally across the bed! At home Princess has her own royal suite, but when we travel, she sleeps with me. Imagine my surprise when she arranged herself on one of the stripes—and slept diagonally for our entire stay! . . . My daughter said I should write to you about this.

about gin gin

While visiting a friend in Paris, I met her cat, Gin Gin, a charming Siamese who presented me with a green feather when we were introduced. It was an obvious compliment, because the feather was his favorite possession. We shared it during my stay. He was always busy with it, carrying it around, putting it in some special place, guarding it, letting me have it for a brief while—a most engaging ritual! But after I returned home, my friend wrote to say that Gin Gin had lost his feather! He was distraught! The apartment had been turned upside down in search of the feather. No luck! Friends brought other feathers in other colors. Gin Gin wanted his own green feather! How to explain this? What to do?

My advice: Consult a psycatatrist. I presumed there would be one in Paris.

13.

do cats have a sense of humor?

I wrote in the "Qwill Pen" column: "Yum Yum has a new and amusing prank. She pulls the bookmark out of the book I'm reading, causing me to lose my place. Very funny! Someday she'll learn how to put it back in the wrong place, and that'll be a real boffo!"

The questions about cats' humor brought such a flood of replies from readers that it was necessary to add to the staff in the mail department. Slitting envelopes, reading the contents, returning the letter in the envelope (a chore in itself), and routing it to me was a time-consuming process until the management decreed that all communications to the "Qwill Pen" must be condensed to fit on a government postal card. As a result, the sale of postal cards became so overwhelming in Moose County post offices that an investigation was thought necessary at one point; it was feared that the cards were being used for some illegal purpose. At the newspaper a part-time assistant is still required to scan and classify the messages. My query about the feline sense of humor brought more responses than any other topic, leading to the conclusion that the sense of humor belongs less to the cat and more to the cat lover. Some examples:

"My cat likes to steal the top of my pen and bury it in his commode. (A scatological joke.) By the time I dredge it out of the kitty gravel, the bottom of the pen has disappeared."

"When I put my hand in my pocket, I never know what I'll find: a grape? . . . a dollar bill that doesn't belong to me? . . . a fur ball? . . . or worse?"

"What is so funny about dragging a toothbrush into the living room when you have company that you're trying to impress?"

"Untying shoelaces has become the national feline pastime. This may explain the trend to loafers."

"The members of our family have lost a total of eleven lipsticks—never found! We think our Tom Tom is operating a black market in cosmetics. Now eye shadow has turned up missing."

"The vibration from heavy truck traffic, the nearby airport, and abandoned mine shafts used to tilt the pictures on the wall— or so we thought, until we caught our roguish tabby in the act."

14.

the day yum yum got out

"Don't let your cats out," the neighbors warned. "There's a cat killer stalking the neighborhood. Raccoon, fox, wild dog—we don't know what it is."

"Don't worry," I said. "My cats don't even go on the screened porch unless I'm in the cabin. If I have to go into town, I lock them up indoors."

It was our first summer in the seventy-five-year-old log cabin. The nearest neighbors were half a mile down the beach. My two city-bred cats were in heaven—watching the wildlife. From the kitchen porch they could see birds, chipmunks, rabbits, and even garden snakes.

The screened porch on the lakeside was

screened on three sides, from floor to ceiling, with a panoramic view of seagulls, grasshoppers, sandpipers—and more chipmunks. Those little striped beasties with twitching noses and flirty tails came right up to the screen to tease Yum Yum.

One afternoon—I'll never forget that day if I live to be a hundred!—I was typing at the dining table. Koko was on the kitchen porch, scolding the wildlife; and Yum Yum was being unusually quiet on the lakeside porch.

Suddenly there was a wrenching, tearing sound! I rushed out in time to see Yum Yum chasing a chipmunk! A corner of the old screening had torn away! And Yum Yum was chasing a chipmunk down the side of the dune, where they both disappeared in the tall beach grass.

I called her name loudly and thrashed through the tall grasses in vain. There was a flash of movement headed east, and I followed on the sandy shore—calling her and watching for movement in the weeds. Occasionally there would be a glimpse of light-and-dark fur, just ahead. At first I was angry! Where did she think she was going? Why didn't she answer my stern calls? Then anger gave way to panic as I thought of the "cat killer"! The heat of anger was replaced by cold sweat. She was so young, so small! She would be helpless! Would she know enough to climb a tree?

I was thrashing around in the beach grass like a madman. I was calling her till I was hoarse.

Then my heart sank as I saw a large brown animal running our way.

I was ready to battle him bare-handed. He stopped near a fallen tree, its rotted trunk broken in pieces. He sniffed it. I yelled at him—some kind of thundering curse— and reached for a branch of the fallen tree. He whimpered and lowered his head as he turned and headed back down the beach.

Only then did I hear a small cry: "Now-w-w!" It was coming from inside the rotting log. Down on my hands and knees I could see her squirming to get out of the hollow log.

All I could say was, "Yum Yum . . . Yum Yum" as I stuffed her inside my shirt and jogged home.

The old screens were immediately re-placed on both porches and eventually I

learned the big brown dog who led me to
shivering Yum Yum was a harmless collie
belonging to one of the cottagers. I apologized to the collie. His name was Robbie.

15.

limericks: fun in the boondocks

I was a precocious fourth-grader when I discovered that rhymed words can be funny, and I started writing slightly naughty couplets about our teachers. Example:

Old Miss Perkins, flat as a pie.
Never had a boyfriend, and we know why.

My chum Arch Riker sold them in the school yard for a penny. Unfortunately, our enterprise was short lived. Now, several decades later, I entertain myself by writing limericks—and encouraging others to do so. "Anyone can write a limerick" is my slogan. And the good folk of Moose County have become writers of rhymed jingles with the traditional five lines in a-a-b-b-a rhyme scheme.

The best limericks focus on a person or a place. The winner of the annual Qwill Pen Limerick Contest celebrated the town of Brrr, coldest in the county, where the lake is said to be frozen ice in winter and melted ice in summer.

There was a young lady from Brrr
Who always went swimming in fur.
One day, on a dare,
She swam in the bare,
And that was the end of her!

Here in the boondocks it's noticeable that animals, wild and domestic, so often are the stars of our limericks:

A sexy young tomcat named Jet
Loved every lady he met.
One day he got ill
And they gave him a pill,
And now he's suing the vet.

A black-and-white stray named Toulouse
Found a home in the county of Moose.
Now he dines on ice cream
And chicken supreme
And oysters and pâté of goose.

An amazing young fellow named Cyril
Was ingenious, agile, and virile.
He ran up and down trees
On his hands and his knees
And eventually married a squirrel.

A sweet little feline named Catta
Is getting fatta and fatta.
But she's very nice
At catching mice
So what do an ounce or two matta?

A bibliocat named Dundee
Is as Scotch as a feline can be.
He quotes Burns quite a lot
And reads Sir Walter Scott
And dines on haggis and tea.

❧

A handsome young feline named Frodo
Is aware of the meaning of no-no.
But he doesn't give a tat
Because he is a CAT
And thinks everyone else is a Dodo.

❧

Old Bubba is not very brave
And hasn't learned how to behave.
But he warns of dangers
And murderous strangers.
And we'll love him from here to the
grave.

❧

A live-in charmer—Miss Kitty—
Is blue-eyed and loving and pretty.
Chasing to and fro
She never says no.
She's a cat, not a girl. What a pity!

16.

cool koko also says

- Dumb animals know more about humans than dumb humans know about animals.

- When the man's away, the cats will play.

- Ring out, wild bells! Here comes the dogcatcher.

- A penny saved . . . isn't worth a sniff of catnip these days.

- A dog by any other name would smell like a dog.

- Half a dish of cream is better than none.

- A cat can look at a king . . . and doesn't have to lick his boots.

- Bite not, lest ye be bitten.

17.

the fine art of
naming cats

What's your cat's name? Ask that question and brighten someone's day. People seem to enjoy telling the names of their pets— and how they came together.

They'll say, "Her name is Snowball. A dear friend in Florida had a litter of kittens and wanted me to have one for old times' sake. The little thing flew north all by herself, and we drove to the Chicago airport to meet her. There she was sitting in a travel coop, quite self-possessed, among all the luggage. She melted our hearts. Her name on the coop was Sunshine, but we thought Snowball was more appropriate. She didn't mind."

Or they'll say, "His name is Pasha. When

we found him, he was an abandoned kitten stuck in a drainpipe and crying his eyes out. At first we called him Little Devil because he was so naughty, but he grew into a lordly member of the family and we call him Pasha."

There are scores of reasons for naming cats. I know a cat in Japan called Mr. Jones, and a cat in Kansas named Hiroshi.

I also know a Siamese who was named Bootsie when he was a kitten because of his little brown feet. When he grew up to be a handsome adult, he appeared to have an emotional problem; he was shy and disagreeable with outsiders. When renamed Brutus, he developed a whole new personality: sophisticated, forthright, and obviously the head of the household.

What's the name of your cat? When readers of the "Qwill Pen" column were asked that question, an avalanche of postal cards descended on the mail room of *The Moose County Something.*

Pinky and Quinky for a pair of longhairs— short for propinquity and equanimity.

Toulouse for a black-and-white long-hair—suggested by the black-and-white posters of the artist Toulouse-Lautrec.

Jet Stream, for the companion of the WPKX weatherman.

Holy Terror, for the obstreperous Siamese living under the same roof as a retired clergyman.

I noted that two-syllable names are in the majority—the better to catch a cat's attention, perhaps. . . . A few names are uncomplimentary—the less said about them, the better. A few are named after famous personages, but they are unwieldy and say more about the cat-person than about the cat. I find nothing catly about Socrates or Babe Ruth. Nor do I approve of calling a cat George or Pauline.

The largest category of cat names submitted by readers were those connected with food. They amuse the humans without offending the pets. Peaches, Pumpkin, Jellybean, Ginger, Pepper, Strudel, and Popcorn.

But he's your cat, and if you want to call him George (after your grandfather) it will be okay with him, as long as you feed him well.

18.

yum yum and the queen-size bed

I'll never forget the trick a delicate little seven-pound cat played on two healthy adult males at the Nutcracker Inn. It had to do with her uncanny sense of spatial relationships.

At home she liked to sit on top of a seven-foot cabinet and watch the scene below without getting involved. She would stand in front of it, look up, crouch, then rise to the top in a fluid leap, propelled by her incredible hind legs. She never fell short and never overshot the mark.

When I had a visitor, Yum Yum would walk into the room just enough to make her presence felt (she liked compliments) but not close enough to be grabbed. Scientists say a cat gauges how far a human can lunge, adjusting for the individual's height and arm length.

One summer I took the Siamese to the Nutcracker Inn for a short vacation. We asked for a cabin near the creek, but it had not been vacated, so they gave us a room in the tower, temporarily.

When it was time to move to the cabin, the porter came up to help with the luggage.

Koko jumped into the carrier, ready to go, but Yum Yum never likes a change of address. She disappeared under the bed. Lying flat on the floor, I tried to grab her, but it was a queen-size bed, and she was positioned under the exact center, beyond reach.

"No problem," said the porter. "The bed's on rollers. I'll pull it to one side, and you grab her."

He pulled, and I grabbed. But Yum Yum moved with the bed, staying under its exact center. He quickly rolled it back into place, and Yum Yum just as quickly stayed in dead center.

"Ignore her," I said. "Start taking the luggage out . . ."

Immediately Yum Yum wriggled out of her hiding place and jumped into the carrier with Koko.

That's what I mean about cats. They're always trying to make fools of us humans.

19.

koko's unique
social graces

Although he has never owned a wristwatch, Koko is keenly aware of time. At eight A.M. sharp he expects breakfast. At twelve noon his midday treat is scheduled—something crunchy, good for his teeth. At six P.M. dinner is served, and it had better be on time. At eleven P.M. it is bedtime snack and lights out.

Occasionally, I invite a friend or two in for drinks and music in the evening. The cats are not in evidence, but at quarter to eleven Koko becomes nervous and parades back and forth through the area where they are seated. If they are not gone by eleven o'clock he presents himself briefly, then turns and walks to the front door, looking back once or twice to see if anyone is following. Two or three of these maneuvers deliver a telepathic message to the guests, who say, "Well, it's time I headed home" or "Thanks for a pleasant evening, Qwill. "

Koko's finest moment occurred, however, on the evening of a cheese-tasting party to benefit the Literacy Council. It was black-tie. Fifty of the best people paid three hundred dollars a ticket for the privilege of tasting cheese and drinking wine in my converted apple barn, considered architecturally spectacular.

At nine o'clock the guests arrived by jitney and gasped at their first view of the barn floodlighted and resembling a medieval castle. Indoors the uplights and downlights dramatized the balconies and ramps . . . the huge fireplace cube in the center of the space, with white stacks rising to a roof forty feet overhead . . . the living areas that surrounded the cube in one breathtaking flow of space.

The guests themselves glittered: the women in family jewels or beaded evening dresses; the men in dinner jackets and diamond studs. They drank amber punch and sampled cheeses from all over the world. Their small talk was witty.

Yum Yum watched from a safe distance, but Koko paraded among the guests, accepting their lavish compliments as his due. If he had owned a wristwatch, he would have been consulting it nervously. Eleven o'clock was approaching, and no one wanted to leave.

Suddenly there was a strange commotion in the kitchen, followed by a thumping and a growling and a loud shattering crash! Conversation stopped abruptly, and I rushed to the kitchen. When I tried to intervene the cat leaped over the bar and crashed into a lamp, sending the shade and the base flying in opposing directions. Women screamed and men yelled as Koko zipped around the fireplace cube and headed for the cheese table, scattering platters of cheese before leaping to the punch table and knocking over the lighted candles.

"Fire!" someone yelled.

"Grab him!"

Three men tore after the mad cat as he

streaked around the fireplace cube with fur flying!

They bumped into furniture and each other.

"Somebody go the other way!"

Somebody did, but the trapped animal only sailed to the top of the fireplace cube and looked down on his pursuers.

"We've got him!"

A moment later Koko swooped over their heads and pelted up the ramp, not stopping till he reached the roof, where he perched on a beam and licked his fur.

I was embarrassed. "My apologies," I said. "The cat went berserk. I don't know why."

Truthfully, I suspected that he wanted everyone to go home. It was, after all, eleven o'clock.

20.

kidnapped!

It was opening night of the new play at the K Theatre, and I was there as the drama critic of the newspaper. During intermission I met Nick and Lori Bamba in the lobby and suggested they come to my place for drinks after the show.

Nick, who had connections with the sheriff's department, said, "There's a stranger in town who's wanted by the police for breaking and entering. He steals radios, cameras, things like that, that he can sell to support his habit, they think. People who've seen him say he wears a beard and drives a purple car. . . . Keep your eyes open!"

"There are quite a few purple cars around here," I said, "and quite a few beards."

After the final curtain, I left the theater before the applause and went home to turn on the lights and prepare for my guests. What I found was the most sickening shock I've ever had! The glass in the back door was broken! Koko's wailing was gut-wrenching, and Yum Yum was missing.

The Bambas arrived, and Nick said, "That's him! That's the suspect. We saw a purple car turning into the shantytown road when we were driving to the theater. Come on! We'll find Yum Yum! I've got a gun in the glove compartment!"

Shantytown was a slum of junk housing, and a purple car was parked alongside an old trailer home. Through the window we could see a bearded man on a cot and stacks of obviously stolen goods. We barged in.

"Freeze!" Nick said, waving the handgun.

"Where's the cat?" I demanded.

"N-n-now!" came a pitiful cry from what looked like a closet.

It was a toilet, and Yum Yum was cowering in the rusty bowl.

While I wrapped her in my jacket, Nick kept the befuddled suspect covered and barked over his shoulder, "Call the police from my cell phone!"

Poor little Yum Yum! What a terrifying experience it must have been. There were bloody scratches on the man's face. Were they her claw marks? Or Koko's?

The morning after . . .

I slept poorly, following the ghastly incident. Rather than relive the harrowing emotions of the night, however, I purposely envisioned the pleasures and chuckles of life with Yum Yum. Koko was such a remarkable cat that I tended to let him dominate the scene. Now, I reviewed Yum Yum's contributions like a series of brief film clips:

Yum Yum on a serious mission: She would walk through the room in a straight line with a resolute step, looking neither to left nor right, ignoring questions and friendly greetings. Her back was as straight as a shelf, and her tail was perfectly horizontal. She knew where she was going, and she went there. She was going to the kitchen for a drink of water.

Yum Yum in a playful mood: She would flop over on the floor and play dead, and I would give her soft underside a gentle nudge with the toe of my shoe. Instantly, she would galvanize into fierce action: coiling around my shoe, grabbing my ankle with her forelegs, and kicking with her hind legs. It was her favorite game.

Yum Yum being amiable: She had several lovable tricks, above and beyond the rubbing of ankles and soulful stares (the little hoyden!). She would snuggle close to my rib cage when I read aloud, purring at the vibrations.

She would reach up with a paw and touch my mustache in wonder. When I lounged at the end of a busy day, she would arrange herself around my neck like a fur collar, finally biting my ear with discretion.

21.

more cool kokoisms

- Every dog has his day. A cat has 365.

- Opportunity knocks only once; grab that pork chop while no one's looking.

- Why sing for your supper? It's easier just to stare at your empty plate.

- Man works from sun till sun, but a cat gets by without lifting a paw.

- To every problem there is a solution: try staring at the handle of the refrigerator.

- Never complain, never explain; just throw up that wet fur ball.

- Art is long; life is short; leave some scratches on the piano.

22.

yum yum discovers her wings

She had lived a sheltered life before joining our household and was slow to emerge from kittenhood until we spent that summer in a log cabin at the beach. Its interior must have looked strange and wonderful, especially the ceiling open to the roof twenty feet overhead, crisscrossed with log beams and rafters. It sparked a primitive urge, and she would never be the same.

Neither would I! I remember it now as my Early Yum Yum Period, which I perpetuated in verse.

I'll always remember Yum Yum
And the way she flew through the air

*Without any wings—just muscles like
springs—
And a will to get where she was going
Without knowing quite where!
One minute she'd be on the mantel,
The next on the rafter up high.
Then down she would swoop, just missing
the soup
Or chili or strawberry pie.
But . . . no matter how bad her behavior,
We forgave her.
She'd prowl around ten feet overhead
And pounce on my stomach as I lay in bed.
At dinnertime she'd slip off a beam
And land with her feet in a dish of ice
cream.
She'd knock over a chair in the middle of
the night,
Break some glasses, give us a fright.
All the while crowing with voice loud and
clear
That would frazzle the nerves and shatter
the ear.
Yes, I'll always remember Yum Yum—
All devil, all angel, all brat.
And not much chin but reckless as sin!
All furry, all purry, all cat!*

Postscript:

Yum Yum is now a poised, grown-up lady cat, but there are times—usually at the full moon — when there is a certain glint in her violet-tinged blue eyes. Is she getting that old feeling?